Penguin Modern Europe...

Advisory Editor: A. Alva...

GW00644859

Selected Poems: Gi...

Giuseppe Ungaretti was the son of Tuscan peasants who
emigrated to Egypt and ran a small bakery in a suburb
of Alexandria. He was born in 1888. It was not until
1912 that Ungaretti left Alexandria. He went to Paris,
and on the way caught his first glimpse of Italy. The
war broke out, and Ungaretti went to Milan, where he
published his first poems in the magazine *Lacerba*.
When Italy entered the war in 1915 he joined up as a
private in the infantry and was sent to the front line on
the Carso. There he was in the thick of some of the
worst fighting of the war. His first small volume was
written in the trenches and published in 1916. These
poems are included in *Allegria* (1919).
Back in Paris after the war, he brought out a volume of
poems in French (*La Guerre*), and married in 1920. He
went to live in Rome the following year, supporting
himself as a journalist. His second major volume,
Sentimento del Tempo (The Feeling of Time), came out in
1933. In 1939 his nine-year-old son Antonietto died,
and Ungaretti's grief is clear in *Il Dolore* (1947). The
most important of his subsequent publications have
been *La Terra Promessa* (1950), *Un Grido e Paesaggi*
(1952), and *Il Taccuino del Vecchio* (1960). In addition he
has translated works of Shakespeare and Blake,
Góngora, Mallarmé, Racine and others.

Selected Poems

Giuseppe Ungaretti

Edited and translated with an Introduction
and Notes by Patrick Creagh

 Penguin Books

Penguin Books Ltd, Harmondsworth,
Middlesex, England
Penguin Books Inc., 7110 Ambassador Road,
Baltimore, Maryland 21207, U.S.A.
Penguin Books Australia Ltd, Ringwood,
Victoria, Australia

The poems by Giuseppe Ungaretti were first
published in the following volumes: *Allegria*
(1919), *Sentimento del Tempo* (1933), *Il Dolore*
(1947), *Il Taccuino del Vecchio* (1960)
Copyright © Arnoldo Mondadori Editore, 1969

First published by Penguin Books 1971
Translations copyright © Patrick Creagh, 1971

Made and printed in Great Britain by
C. Nicholls & Company Ltd
Set in Monotype Garamond

Contents

Introduction

Giuseppe Ungaretti was the son of Tuscan peasants who emigrated to Egypt and ran a small bakery in a suburb of Alexandria. It was there that Ungaretti was born, on 10 February 1888. Two years later his father was killed while working on the Suez Canal diggings, but his mother kept on the bakery until 1906. It was not until 1912 that Ungaretti left Alexandria.

He went to Paris and, on the way, caught his first glimpse of Italy. Paris was still in its heyday, so his introduction to the European cultural scene was a characteristically intensive one.

The war broke out and Ungaretti went to Milan, where he published his first poems in the magazine *Lacerba*. When Italy entered the war in 1915 he joined up as a private in the infantry and was sent to the front line on the Carso. There he was in the thick of some of the worst fighting of the war. His first small volume, *Il Porto Sepolto* (The Buried Harbour), was written in the trenches and published (eighty copies) in 1916. These poems are included in *Allegria* (1919).

Back in Paris after the war, he brought out a volume of poems in French (*La Guerre*), and married in 1920. He went to live in Rome the following year, supporting himself as a journalist. His second major volume, *Sentimento del Tempo* (The Feeling of Time), came out in 1933 and in 1936 he went to Brazil as Professor of Italian at São Paolo. In 1939 his nine-year-old son Antonietto died of appendicitis. *Il Dolore* (Grief), published in 1947, must be read in the light of this tragic personal event. The most important of his subsequent publications have been *La Terra Promessa*

(1950), *Un Grido e Paesaggi* (1952), and *Il Taccuino del Vecchio* (1960). In addition he has translated works of Shakespeare and Blake, Góngora, Mallarmé, Racine and others.

This kind of summary can scarcely touch on the *life* of a poet, let alone such a one as Ungaretti, who referred to his early war poems – the ones that made him famous – as 'a kind of diary', and gave his poetry as a whole the collective title of *Vita d'un uomo*. But there are circumstances and events that any reader of his poetry must bear in mind: Ungaretti's birth and upbringing in Egypt and an education that was more French than Italian; the experiences of the First World War in which he fought and wrote; the death of his son. From his earliest printed works to the latest included here, we feel that whenever Ungaretti mentions a desert it is more to him than a metaphor. Desert scenes and feelings arise spontaneously in him, part of his whole apprehension of the world. Alexandria, for Ungaretti, was a city that 'time is forever carrying away, at all times. It is a city where the feeling of time, of time the destroyer, is present before and above all.' He is speaking of Alexandria as though it were his own poetry.

Another, if less profound, effect of his foreign birth was felt in his earliest literary influences. He spoke French as a mother tongue, and was drawn to the French poets he read as a schoolboy, particularly Baudelaire and Mallarmé. When he started writing in Italian he was free of the literary squabbles of Italian poetry and did not need to commit himself to any current, or even think of doing so. He started clean of slavish and modish ways that would have blunted the immediacy of his talent.

And it was nothing, if not immediate. The earliest work of most poets is imitative, because poets are self-taught, and only with maturity do they sometimes find their own unmistakable idiom. Ungaretti is a teasing exception. In his first book he was already totally himself, making an entirely new sound in Italian.

During the war, with not much time to spare in the trenches, Ungaretti came out with a poetry that was miniature, simple, stripped to the feeling bone. It was based on a magic touch with language and unabashed truthfulness to the experience. A famous and untranslatable example is 'Mattina' (Morning):

> M'illumino
> d'immenso

That's the lot. And this is one of Ungaretti's war poems, which have in them less bitterness and more love of life than most poets could manage if they were basking at ease in Eden, instead of under gunfire.

Spontaneous, simple, very condensed but without pretension, Ungaretti's poetry cut rhetoric dead. All the emphasis was on the word itself, each word, its sound, meaning, resonance, and the space it could be made to fill.

Ungaretti at this time was not ignorant of Italian literature: Leopardi and Petrarca were two of his most revered masters. But he came to it with an unscholastic freshness and an eye for what he wanted. It was their song he was after: *cercavo in loro il canto*.

The impact of the tradition on Ungaretti can be seen in the 'very slow distillation' that was his second volume, *Sentimento del Tempo* (1919–33). The measure is now the phrase, not the single word. The verse is far more sensuous and complex. In almost everything he writes there is a landscape, a real landscape (usually that of the Roman *campagna*) that is also an image of a state or movement of feeling. The verse has the weight and heat and also the languor and

9

savagery, of summer. Summer is everywhere in these poems: 'During those years I only managed to grasp nature when it was at the sun's mercy and the travertine was burning . . . '

What 'summer' means to Ungaretti is not entirely sensuous. July 'goes stripping the earth's skeleton'. In much the same way, when Ungaretti begins to write on religious themes ('Pity', p. 79) it is not on the comforting, sensuous or ecstatic aspects of piety that he dwells, but on the emptiness, the deprivation, the absence of God in us. At the same time he was discovering Rome, where he was now living. This discovery meant coming to terms with the baroque, and 'the baroque arouses the sense of the void'.

Such themes run through the poems of *Sentimento del Tempo*. With this book, all the critics agree, Ungaretti had moved into a new phase, and he was climbing the ladder of invention as neatly as any of them could have wished. But the thing broke under him. His young son died and he felt guilt as well as sorrow. The poems of *Il Dolore* (1947) remained especially personal and painful; they had unique value for him, but he was unable even to comment on them. The war and the tragedy of Italy that coincided with their composition reinforced the note of desperation in them.

The first inklings of *La Terra Promessa* came in about 1935, but this work was interrupted by the experience of *Il Dolore* and was published unfinished in 1950. Here it was autumn that Ungaretti wished to celebrate: 'a late autumn, from which the last signs of youth, of earthly youth, and the last appetites of the flesh, are departing for ever'.

There is nothing strained or conventional about Ungaretti's identification of the phases of his life with the seasons of the year. He simply followed his moods, in this as in all things, trusting in his instincts to find fit language. When he cannot find it, he knows and laments the fact ('In

My Veins'). Though far from ingenuous, he was a genuine innocent. You will find sorrow and suffering, guilt and remorse in his works, but not bitterness or cynicism. He was as incapable of bearing a grudge against life as against an individual, and incapable of hate. In spite of proclaiming himself *uomo di pena*, man of sorrows, he was a poet of joy.

Eternal

Between one flower picked and the other given
the inexpressible nothing

Ennui

Even tonight will pass

This wandering solitude
wavering shadow of tramwires
on the damp asphalt

I watch the heads of cabbies
in a doze
lolling

Levant*

The line of smoke
dies out upon
the distant ring of the sky

Clatter of heels clapping of hands
and the clarinet's shrill flourishes
and the sky is ashen
trembles gentle uneasy
like a dove

In the stern Syrian emigrants are dancing

In the bow a young man is alone

On Saturday evenings at this time
Jews
in those parts
carry away
their dead
through the shell's spiralling
uncertainties
of alleyways
of lights

Churning of water
like the racket from the stern
that I hear within the shadow
of
sleep

*Ungaretti is leaving his birthplace of Alexandria on his way to
France. 'In those parts' refers to Alexandria.

Carpet

Each colour expands and stretches out
into the other colours

To be the more alone if you look at it

Maybe a River*

There is the mist that blots us out

Maybe a river is born up here

I listen to the Sirens' song
from the lake where the city was

*Ungaretti explains that the mist had changed Milan into a lake that
'like a mirage' reminded him of the lake of Mareotis, near Alexandria.

Agony

To die like thirsty larks
upon the mirage

Or as the quail
the sea once past
having no more
will to fly
dies in the first thickets

But not to live on lamentation
like a blinded goldfinch

Memory of Africa

The sun snatches the city away

We can no longer see

Not even the graves hold out for long

In a Tunnel

An eye of stars
peers at us from that pool
and filters down its icy benediction
to this aquarium
of sleep-walking boredom

Chiaroscuro

Even the graves have vanished

Black infinite space draped
from this balcony
down to the graveyard

And it occurred to me to visit
my Arab friend
who killed himself the other evening

Day again

The graves return
crouching in the dismal green
of the last darkness
in the troubled green
of the first light

A People*

I fled from the lonely herd of palms
and the moon
infinite over barren nights

The most enclosed of nights
lugubrious turtle
gropes

No colour lasts

The drunken pearl of doubt
already moves the dawn and
at its momentary feet
embers

The cries of a new wind
are already swarming

Stream-beds are hidden in the hills
of vanished fanfares

Return you ancient mirrors
you hidden water's edges

And
while the sharp young shoots
of the high snows border
the view my fathers used to see
the sails align
in the clear calm

*On his way to France, Ungaretti caught his first glimpse of Italy.

O my country every age of yours
wakens in my blood

Confidently you advance and sing
over a starving sea

In Memoriam

Locvizza, 30 September 1916

He was called
Mohammed Sheab

Descendant of nomad emirs
a suicide
because he no longer had
a country

He loved France
and changed his name

Became Marcel
but was not French
and had forgotten how
to live
in his own people's tent
where they listen to the sing-song
of the Koran
as they sip coffee

He did not know
how to release
the song
of his unconstraint

I followed his coffin
I and the manageress of the hotel
where we lived
in Paris

number 5 rue des Carmes
steep decrepit alleyway

He rests
in the cemetery at Ivry
a suburb that always
looks
like the day
they dismantle a fairground

And perhaps only I
still know
he lived

The Buried Harbour*

Mariano, 29 June 1916

The poet goes there
then returns to the light with his songs
and scatters them

Of this poetry
there remains to me
that nothing
of inexhaustible secrecy

*This is the title poem of a small but very important book, published
in 1916. It contained the poems written in Ungaretti's first year of war.

Clear Desert Gold*

Cima Quattro, 22 December, 1915

Sway of smoking wings
cuts short the eyes' silence

The wind snaps off the coral buds
of a thirst for kisses

I gape at dawn

Life is poured out for me
in a whirlpool of nostalgias

Now I mirror those corners of the world
I had for companions
and sniff out my way

Even unto death at the mercy of our journey

We have the truces of sleep

The sun dries tears

I cover myself with a warm cloak
of clear gold

From this shelf of desolation
I lean into the arms
of the good weather

*Original title – 'Lindoro di deserto'. Ungaretti explains: 'Lindoro is one of the characters of the Venetian masques; the word indicates both the poet himself and the effect of sun described in the poem.'

'This shelf of desolation'; the poem was written on 'Cima Quattro', i.e. 'Hill 4' – on the front line.

W atch

A whole night through
thrown down beside
a butchered comrade
with his clenched teeth
turned to the full moon
and the clutching
of his hands
thrust
into my silence
I have written
letters full of love

Never have I
clung
so fast to life

On Leave
Versa, 27 April 1916

Who will come with me through the fields

The sun scatters itself in diamond
drops of water
on the pliant grass

I fall in with
the pleasure
of the calm-hearted universe

The mountains swell
in draughts of lilac shadow
and row along with the sky

In the light vault above
the spell has broken

And I plummet into myself

And hide in a nest within myself

Sunset

Versa, 20 May 1916

The sky's flushed face
wakens oases
for love's nomad

Annihilation

Versa, 21 May 1916

The heart has been prodigal of fireflies
has flared and died
from green to green
I have numbered the pulses

With my two hands I mould the soil
scattered with crickets
I tune myself
to a heart
subdued and steady

She loves me she loves me not
I have enamelled myself
with daisies
I have put down roots
into the rotten earth
I have grown
like a poppy
on its twisted stem
I have gathered myself
in the fall
of hawthorn

Today
like the Isonzo
river of blue asphalt
I settle down
in the ashes of its gravel bed
bared by the sun

and change
into a flight of clouds

Fully at last
unleashed
the usual self surprised
no longer beats the rhythm of the heart
has neither time nor place
is happy

On my lips I have
the kiss of marble

Suspended Moment*

Mariano, 25 June 1916

March on march on
I have found the well
of love again

In the eye
of a thousand-and-one-nights
I have rested

In the abandoned gardens
she came in to rest
like a dove

In the fainting
midday air
I picked
for her
oranges and jasmine

*Original title – 'Fase'.

Silence

Mariano, 27 June 1916

I know a city
that every day fills to the brim with sunlight
and in that instant everything is enchanted

I left one evening

In my heart the rasp of the cicadas
went on

From the white
painted vessel
I saw
my city disappear
leaving
an embrace of lights
for a while
in the troubled air
hanging

Burden

Mariano, 29 June 1916

That peasant
trusts in his
St Antony medal
and walks lightly

But bone-naked
on its own
without mirage
I bear my soul

Awakenings

Mariano, 29 June 1916

Each moment
I have lived
once before
in a deep epoch
outside myself

I am far off with memory
following those lost lives

I awake in a bath
of cherished accustomed things
surprised
and sweetened

I chase clouds that
softly dissolve
with watchful eyes
and I remember
some dead friend

But what is God ?

And the terrified
creature opens
wide its eyes
and welcomes
drops of stars
and the dumb plain

And feels
restored

Brothers

Mariano, 15 July 1916

What regiment are you from
brothers ?

Word trembling
in the night

A leaf just opening

In the racked air
involuntary revolt
of man face to face with his own
fragility

Brothers

I Am Alive

Valloncello di Cima Quattro, 5 August 1916

Like this stone
of Monte San Michele
as cold as this
as hard as this
as dried as this
as stubborn as this
as utterly
dispirited as this

Like this stone
is my unseen
weeping

Death
we discount
by living

My Rivers

I cleave to this mutilated tree
forsaken in this hollow
that is as lifeless
as a circus
between performances
and I watch
the clouds pass
quietly across the moon

This morning I stretched out
in an urn of water
and like a relic
rested

The Isonzo polished me
in its current
like one of its own stones

I hoisted myself
up and went
like an acrobat
over the water

I squatted down
near my clothes
foul with war
and like a bedouin
bowed down to receive
the sun

This is the Isonzo
and here I have
best known myself to be
an obedient nerve
of the universe

My torture is
not to believe myself
in harmony

But those hidden
hands that knead me
give to me
the rarest
happiness

I have reviewed
the ages
of my life

These are
my rivers

This is the Serchio*
which has given water
for two thousand years maybe
to my peasant people
to my father and my mother

This is the Nile
that saw me
born and growing
burning with ignorance
in the wide plains

*The Serchio flows near Lucca.

This is the Seine
and in its turbulence
I have been stirred
and come to know myself

These are my rivers
summed up in the Isonzo

This is my nostalgia
that shines through to me
in each of them
now that it is night
that my life seems to me
a corolla
of shadows

Monotony

Valloncello dell'Albero Isolato, 22 August 1916

Halted at two stones
I weaken
beneath this
blurred vault
of sky

The tangle of paths
crowds my blindness

There is nothing meaner
than this monotony

At one time
I did not know
that even
the way the sky
fades at evening
is just an
ordinary thing

And upon my soothed
African soil
with an arpeggio
lost in the air
I was renewed

The Clear Night

Devetachi, 24 August 1916

What song has risen tonight
to weave
the heart's crystal echo with
the stars

What feast has risen
from rejoicing heart

I have been
a pool of darkness

Now like a child at the nipple
I bite at
space

Now I am drunk with
universe

Sleepiness

From Devetachi to San Michele, 25 August 1916

These hump-backed hills
have gone to bed
in the darkness of the valleys

Now nothing reaches me
there is nothing left
but a rattle of crickets

That keeps step
with my troubled thoughts

Clash

Locvizza, 23 September 1916

With my wolf's hunger
I pull down
my lamb's body

I am like
the helpless boat
and like the letching ocean

Nostalgia

Locvizza, 28 September 1916

When
night is almost over
a little before spring starts
and people
seldom pass

A dark colour
of weeping
thickens over Paris

At the corner
of a bridge
I contemplate
the boundless silence
of a slender girl

Our two
maladies
run together

And as if carried somewhere else
there we stay

Why?
Carsia Guilia, 1916

My dark lost heart
needs some relief

In the muddy clefts of rocks
like a grass-blade belonging here
it wants to tremble gently in the light

But I am
in the sling of time
only the chips of crumbling stone
on the makeshift road
of war

Ever since
he looked into the immortal
face of the world
this madman
falling into the labyrinth
of his vexed heart
has longed to know

My listening heart
has been packed down
like a wheel-rut
but found that it was following
the wake
of a dead journey

I watch the horizon
scabbed with craters

My heart wants to flare
at least as tonight does
at least with the jet of rockets

I carry a heart
that thunders underground
and shatters
like a shell
on the plain
but does not leave me with
even a hint of flight

Poor heart
stunned
with unknowing

Envoi*

Locvizza, 2 October 1916

Dear
Ettore Serra
poetry
is the world the human race
my own life
all flowered from the word
the transparent wonder
of a delirious ferment

When I find
one single word
in this my silence
it is hewn into my life
like an abyss

*This is the last poem in *Il Porto Sepolto* and is addressed to Ettore Serra, who published the book.

Gully at Night

Naples, 26 December 1916

Tonight's
face
is dry
as a piece of
parchment

This nomad
bent
softened with snow
lets go
like a curled up
leaf

Unending time
makes use of me
as a
rustle

Solitude

Santa Maria La Longa, 26 January 1917

But my cries
strike
like thunder
on the faint vault
of the sky

They fall back
terrified

Distant

Versa, 15 February 1917

Distant into a distant land
like a blind man
they have led me by the hand

Transfiguration[*]
Versa, 16 February 1917

I stand
my back to a stack of
bronzed hay

An acrid spasm
breaks and swarms
from the rich furrows

Well-born I feel myself to be
sprung from people of the soil

I feel myself behind the eyes
of the man as gnarled
as the bark
of the mulberry-trees he lops

Eyes attentive to
the phases of the sky

Feel myself
in the children's faces
like flushed fruit
burning
among the naked trees

Like a cloud
I am clarified
in sunlight

[*]Ungaretti's emotional discovery of his roots in Italy, and especially among the Tuscan peasantry, is a theme he returns to several times.

I feel dispersed
in a kiss
that consumes me
and calms me

Pleasure

Versa, 18 February 1917

I burn with the
fever
of this spate of light

I welcome this
day like
a sweetening fruit

Tonight
I shall feel
remorse like a
howl
lost in the
desert

Another Night

Vallone, 20 April 1917

In this dark
with frozen hands
I make out
my face

I see myself
adrift in infinite space

*June**

Campolongo, 5 July 1917

When
will this night
die for me
and I like any other
be able to look at it
and go to sleep
to the hush
of the waves
that make their last
somersault
under the mimosa wall
around my house

When again will I wake
in your body
various
as the voice of the nightingale

It stretches out
like the shining
colour of ripe wheat

In the translucency
of water
the tissued gold
of your skin
will be frosted with blackness

*Images of Alexandria are mixed with those of the battlefield.

Poised
on the ringing
flagstones
of the air
you will be
like a panther

In the shifting
edges
of the shade
you will shed your leaves

Raging
dumbly in
that dust
you will smother me

Then
you will half close your eyes

We shall see our love lie down
like evening

Calm again
I shall see
your pupils die to me
on the bitumen horizon
of your eyes

Now
the sky has closed
as
at this time
in my home in Africa
the jasmine does

I have lost the way to sleep

I waver
at a street-corner
like a firefly

Will tonight
die for me

Futility
Vallone, 19 August 1917

Suddenly
high
above the rubble
spreads the crystal
wonder
of boundless space

And the man
bent
over the water
startled
by the sun
comes back to his senses
as a shadow

Cradled and
gradually
crushed

Clear Sky

Bois de Courton, July 1918

After so much
mist
one
by one
the stars
unveil

I breathe in
the cool air
that the colour of the sky
gives me

I know I am
a passing
image

Caught in an immortal
circle

Lucca*

At my home in Egypt, after dinner, when we had said the
rosary, my mother used to tell us about these places.

My childhood was enchanted by them.

Life in this town is pious and fanatical.

One is never inside these walls except in passing.

The aim here is to get away.

I sit outside the restaurant door with people who
speak of California as if it were their farm.

I am terrified at discovering myself in the features of
these people.

Now I feel the blood of my dead run hot in my veins.

I too have swung a mattock.

In the steaming thighs of the earth I find I am
laughing.

Farewell desires, nostalgias.

I know of past and future as much as a man can know.

Now I know my destined end, and my beginnings.

There is nothing left for me to desecrate, nothing to
long for.

I have enjoyed everything, and suffered.

There is nothing for it but to come to terms with
death.

I shall therefore quietly raise a progeny.

When a malignant hunger forced me into mortal
loves, I praised life.

Now that I, even I, think of love as a guarantee of the
species, I have death in mind.

*In this poem Ungaretti openly shows the influence of his friend
Apollinaire. (The line beginning 'I know of past and future' is
virtually copied from *La jolie rousse*). But he soon dropped this manner.

O Night

1919

The vast anxiety of dawn
Reveals the web of branches.

Sorrowful awakenings.

Leaves, sister leaves,
I listen to your lamenting.

Autumns,
Dying sweetnesses.

O youth,
The time of setting out is scarcely over.

High skies of youth,
Unbridled onrush.

And already I am forsaken.

Lost in this stooping melancholy.

But night scatters distances.

Oceanic silences,
Star-nests of illusion,

O night.

Landscape

1920

Morning
She has a garland of fresh thoughts,
Shines in the flowered water.

Afternoon
The mountains have dwindled to thin wisps and the
encroaching desert swarms with impatiences and even
sleep troubles and even the statues are troubled.

Evening
Catching fire she sees that she is naked, the flushed
complexion of the sea gone bottle green, it is nothing but
mother-of-pearl.
That pang of shame in things justifies human sorrow,
revealing for a moment the ceaseless wasting away of all
that is.

Night
Everything is stretched out, thinned out, confused.
Whistles of departing trains.
And here, now there are no longer witnesses,
my own true face appears, weary and disappointed.

Silence in Liguria

1922

A sinuously receding plain of water.

Still out of sight the sun
Bathes in its urns.

A colour of soft flesh passes across.

And suddenly she opens
The great calm of her eyes towards the bays.

The sunken shadow of the rocks dies.

Sweetness budding out from joyful hips,
True love is a gentle kindling,

And I enjoy her
Suffused by the alabaster wing
Of an immobile morning.

Concerning July

1931

When she hurls herself upon us
The brave foliage becomes
A sad rose colour.

She melts ravines, drinks rivers,
Mangles rocks, shines,
She is a rage that never weakens, she is implacable,
She scatters space, blinds purposes,
She is summer and throughout the centuries
With her calcinating eyes
She goes stripping the earth's skeleton.

Juno

1931

Round to that perfect ripeness that torments me,
One thigh rising from upon the other . . .

Scatter your fury through one pungent night!

Concerning August

1925

Hungry mourning buzz among the living,

Monotonous high-seas,
But without solitude,

Muffled fanfares from prostrated harvests,

Summer,

You strip the flints right to their dusky sockets,

You waken ashes in the colosseums . . .

What Erebus shrieked you?

Each Shade of Grey

1925

From the snake's sloughed skin
To the timorous mole
Each shade of grey lingers on the cathedrals . . .

Like a gilded ship the sun
Takes leave of star after star
And frowns under the pergola . . .

Like a tired forehead
Night has reappeared
In the hollow of a hand . . .

It Will Wake You

1931

Beautiful moment, come back close to me.

Speak to me, youth,
At this engulfing hour.

Good thought, sit down a moment.

The hour of black light in the veins
And of dumb shrieks in mirrors,
Of the treacherous precipices of thirst . . .

And from the basest, blindest dust
Comes the promise of the golden age:

With the softness of first steps
When the sun
Has touched the night-earth
Dissolving every pall into freshness,
Returning paler to the skies
A joyous body will wake you.

A Breeze

1927

Hearing the sky
Sword of morning,
And the hill that climbs into its lap,
I return to the accustomed harmony.

A weary clump of trees
Grasps the slope at its foot.

From the mesh of branches
I see flights reborn . . .

Stars

1927

The fables come to blaze again on high.

They will fall with the leaves at the first wind.

But let the next gust come,
New lustres will return.

Spring of Water

1927

The sky has already grown too pale
And now comes shining back
And sows the spring with eyes.

Awakened viper,
Slender idol, stripling river,
Soul, summer come back by night,
The sky is dreaming.

Pray then, I love to hear you,
Changeful grave.

Quiet

1929

The grapes are ripe, the field ploughed,

The hill severs from the clouds.

On summer's dusty mirrors
Shadow has fallen,

Between uncertain fingers
Their gleam is clear,
And distant.

With the swallows flies
The last anguish.

Evening

1929

At the foot of the ravines of evening
Runs a clear
Olive-coloured stream,

And reaches the brief forgetful fire.

Now in the smoke I hear crickets and frogs,

Where tenderly tremble the grasses.

The Captain*

1929

I was ready for any departure.

When you have secrets, night, you have pity too.

If as a child I woke
With a start, it calmed me
To hear stray dogs howling
In the absent street. They seemed to me
More so even than the lamp that burned
Always before the Madonna in that room,
Mystical company.

And by chasing echoes
From before my birth,
Was I not amazed at heart, a man?

But when, O night, your face was bare
And flung down on stone
I was nothing but an elemental nerve,
Maddened, manifest in every object,
Humility was crushing.

The Captain was serene.

(The moon came into the sky)

*Another poem in which memories of childhood and war are mingled. 'Echoes/From before my birth': the poet's ancestors from Lucca. 'And flung down on stone' evokes the landscape of war. 'The Captain' may be given a legendary aura, but he really existed as one Nazzareno Cremona, of Ungaretti's regiment.

He was tall and never stooped.

(A cloud passed across it)

No one saw him fall,
No one heard him groan,
He reappeared stretched in a furrow,
His hands were crossed on his chest.

I closed his eyes.

(The moon is a veil)

He seemed winged.

Where the Light

1930

Like a buoyant thrush
In the happy wind above young meadows,
My arms know you are light, come.

We will forget this world,
Its ills and curses and the sky,
And my blood that is quick to war,
Forget those passes mindful of shadow
In the flush of new mornings.

Where the light no longer moves a leaf,
Our dreams and troubles gone to other shores,
Where evening rests,
Come I will lead you
To the hills of gold.

Free from age, time being still,
In its lost halo
Will our sheet be.

Pity*

1928

I

I am a wounded man.

And I wish to leave this place
And arrive at last,
Pity, where that man is heard
Who is alone with himself.

I have nothing but goodwill and pride.

I feel in exile in the midst of men.

Yet I am suffering for their sake.
Am I unworthy to return into myself?

I have peopled the silence with names.

Have I cut heart and mind to pieces
Only to fall under a yoke of words?

I reign over ghosts.

O dead leaves,
Soul wafted here and there . . .

No, I hate the wind and its
Immemorial beast's voice.

*Ungaretti refers to this poem as the first definite sign of his return
to the Christian faith.

God, do those who implore you
Only know you now by name?

You have driven me out from life.

Will you drive me out from death?

Man is perhaps unworthy even to hope.

Has even the spring of remorse dried up?

What does sin matter
If it no longer leads to purity?

The flesh scarcely remembers
That once it was strong.

Maddened and worn out, the soul.

God, look upon our weakness.

We would ask for something certain.

Do you no longer even laugh at us?

Lament us then, O cruelty.

I can no longer bear to stay walled up
In desire without love.

Show us some token of justice.

What is your law?

Strike with your lightning at my wretched feelings,
Free me from anguish.

I am sick of shrieking soundlessly.

2

Grieving flesh
That at one time teemed with joy,
Half-closed eyes of a tired awakening,
Over-ripened soul, do you see
What I shall be, once fallen into the earth?

Through the living runs the road of the dead,

We ourselves are the crowding shades,

They are the seed that bursts for us in dreams,

Theirs is the distance that is left to us,

Theirs is the shadow that gives weight to names.

The hope of a mound of shade
And nothing more, is that our destiny?

And are you nothing but a dream, O God?

Reckless as we are, we want you
At least to be like a dream.

That is born of clearest madness.

It does not flutter in clouds of branches

Like morning sparrows
At the eyelids' edges.

It remains and rots in us, a mysterious wound.

3
The light that pierces us
Is an ever finer thread.

Do you no longer dazzle, without killing?

Grant me this supreme joy.

4
Man, monotonous universe,
Thinks he is piling up his goods
And from his feverish hands
Only endings endlessly emerge.

Strung over the void
On his spider's thread
He fears nothing and attracts
Nothing but his own cry.

He makes good the waste by raising tombs,
And to speak of you, Eternal One,
Has to use swearwords.

Death Meditated On

1932

First Canto

O sister of shadow,
The fiercer the light is, the more a thing of night,
You pursue me, death.

In a perfect garden
Innocent longing gave birth to you
And peace was lost,
Pensive death,
On your mouth.

Ever since that instant
I have heard you in the mind's flow
Probing distances,
You who copy the eternal one, but suffer.

Venomous mother of the ages
In the fear of the pulse
And of solitude,

Beauty tormented and laughing,

In the drowsing of the flesh
A fugitive dreamer,

Unsleeping athlete
Of our greatness,

When you have tamed me, say:

Through the misery of living men
Will my shade's flight be long?

Second Canto

The dark vigil of our forefathers
Gouges the inner lives
Of our unhappy mask
(Cloister of the infinite)
With fanatic flattery.

Death, dumb word,
Sand like a bed laid down
By the blood,
I hear you sing like a cicada
In the tarnished rose of reflections.

Third Canto

The endless mockery of our forefathers
Cuts the secret furrows
In our unhappy mask.

You in the deep light,
O troubled silence,
Persist like the irascible cicadas.

Fourth Canto

Clouds took me by the hand.

On the hill I burn up space and time,
Like one of your messengers,
Like a dream, sacred death.

Fifth Canto

You have closed your eyes.

A night is born
Full of sham hollows,
Of dead sounds
As of the corks
Of nets dropped in the water.

Your hands become like a breeze
From inviolable distances,
Intangible as ideas

And the ambiguity of the moon
And its rocking, gentlest things.
If you lay those hands upon my eyes
They touch my soul.

You are the woman who passes
Like a leaf

And you leave the trees a blaze of autumn.

Sixth Canto

O lovely quarry,
Voice of night,
Your movements
Rouse a fever.

Only you, crazed memory,
Could have imprisoned liberty.

On your flesh, intangible

And wavering in troubled mirrors,
What crimes, O dream, did you not
Teach me to consummate?

With you, my ghosts, I never have restraint,

And when day comes my heart is full
Of your remorse.

Song

1932

Again I see your slow mouth
(The sea flows to meet it in the night)
And the mare of your loins
Hurling you in agony
Into my singing arms,
And a sleep retrieving you
To coloured things and new deaths.

And the cruel solitude
That every lover finds within himself,
Now an endless grave,
Divides me from you for ever.

Dear one, distant as in a mirror . . .

Weightless

1934

For a God who laughs like a child,
So many cries of sparrows,
So many dances in the boughs,

A soul makes itself weightless,
The meadows take on such a tenderness,
Such modesty rekindles in the eyes,

The hands like leaves
Are spellbound in the air . . .

Who fears any more, who judges?

Day by Day*

1940–46

1

'No one, mother, has ever suffered so . . .'
And the face already dead
But still the living eyes
Turned from the pillow towards the window,
And sparrows filled the room
Coming for the crumbs the father scattered
To distract his child . . .

2

Now only in dreams will I be able
To kiss those trusting hands . . .
And I talk, I work,
I've scarcely changed, I smoke, I am afraid . . .
How is it I stand up to so much night? . . .

3

The years will bring me
God knows what other horrors,
But if I felt you by me
You would console me . . .

4

Never, you will never know how it fills me with light,

*A series of fragments written at various times after the death of the
poet's nine-year-old son in 1939.

89

The shade that comes and stands beside me, shyly,
When I no longer hope . . .

5

Where is it now, where is the innocent voice
That running and resounding from room to room
Raised a tired man from his troubles? . . .
The earth has spoilt it, it is protected by
A past of fairytales . . .

6

Every other voice is a fading echo
Now that one voice calls me
From the immortal heights . . .

7

In the sky I seek your happy face,
And may these eyes of mine see nothing else
When God wills it that they too shall close . . .

8

And I love you, love you, and it is an endless wrenching! . . .

9

Ferocious earth, monstrous sea
Divide me from the place where the grave is
Where that tormented body
Now wastes away . . .
It doesn't matter. . . . Ever more distinctly

I hear that voice of soul
That I failed to succour here below . . .
More joyful and more friendly
As the minutes pass,
It isolates me in its simple secret . . .

10

I have gone back to the hills, to the beloved pines,
And the homely accent of the wind's rhythm
That I will hear no more with you
Breaks me with every gust . . .

11

The swallow passes and summer with her
And I too, I tell myself, will pass . . .
But of the love that rends me may some sign
Remain, apart from this brief misting-over,
If from this hell I reach some kind of peace . . .

12

Under the axe the disenchanted branch
Falls with scarcely a complaint, less
Even than the leaf at the breeze's touch . . .
And it was fury that cut down the tender
Form, and the eager
Compassion of a voice consumes me . . .

13

Summer brings me no more furies,
Nor spring its forebodings;

You can go your way, autumn
With your idiot splendours:
For a desire stripped bare, winter
Extends the gentlest season! . . .

14

Already the drought of autumn
Has sunk into my bones,
But, drawn out by the shadows,
There survives an endless
Demented splendour:
The secret torment of the twilight buried
In an abyss . . .

15

Will I always recall without remorse
A bewitching agony of the senses?
Blind man, listen: 'A spirit has departed
Still unharmed by the common lash of life . . .'

Will I be less cast down to hear no more
The living cries of his innocence
Than to feel almost dead in me
The dreadful shudder of guilt?

16

In the dazzle blaring from the windows
Shade frames a reflection on the tablecloth,
In the faint lustre of a jar the swollen
Hydrangeas from the flower-bed, a drunken swift,
The skyscraper in a blaze of clouds,
A child rocking on a bough, return to mind . . .

92

Inexhaustible thunder of the waves
Forces upon me then, invades the room
And, on the uneasy stillness of a blue
Horizon, all the walls dissolve . . .

17

Mild weather, and perhaps you pass close by
Saying: 'May this sun and so much space
Calm you. In the pure wind you can hear
Time walking, and my voice.
Little by little I have closed and gathered
The mute impulse of your hope in me.
For you I am the dawn and the unbroken day.'

Bitter Chiming

Or else on an October afternoon
From the harmonious hills
Amongst thick lowering clouds
The horses of the Heavenly Twins,
At whose hoofs a boy
Had paused enchanted,
Over storm-water launched

(By a bitter chiming of memories
Towards shadows of banana trees
And of giant turtles
Lumbering between masses
Of vast impassive waters:
Under a different order of stars
Among unfamiliar seagulls)

Their flight to the level place where the boy
Rummaging in the sand –
The transparency of his beloved fingers
Wet with driven rain
Turned to flame by splendour of the lightning –
Clutched all four elements.

But death is colourless and without senses
And ignorant of any law, as ever,
Already grazed him
With its shameless teeth.

You Were Broken

The many grey, monstrous, scattered stones
Still shuddering in the hidden slings
Of stifled primal flames
Or in the terrors of virgin floods
Crumbling in implacable embraces,
– Don't you remember them, on a void horizon
Rigid above the dazzle of the sand?

And leaning, and spreading at the only
Meeting-place of shade in the whole valley,
The monkey-puzzle, breathless, overbloated,
Wound in the arduous flint of lonely fibres,
More stubborn even than the other damned,
Its mouth cool with butterflies and grasses
Where it tore itself from its own roots,
– Don't you remember it, delirious mute
Upon a rounded stone one foot across
In perfect balance
Magically there?

From branch to branch light firecrest
Avid eyes drunk with wonder
You reached its dappled peak,
Reckless one, child of music,
Only to see once more in the last light
Of a deep still sea-chasm
Legendary turtles
Stirring amongst the seaweed.

Nature's utmost tension
And underwater pageants,
Funereal warnings.

2

You raised your arms like wings
And gave rebirth to the wind
Running in the heaviness of the still air.

No one ever saw you rest
Your light dancer's foot.

3

Grace, happy thing,
In such a hardened blindness
How could you not be broken?
You, simple breath and crystal,

A flash of light too human for the savage,
Pitiless, frenzied, throbbing
Roar of a naked sun.

In My Veins

Desire still riding hard in my veins
That by now are almost empty tombs,
In my freezing bones the stone,
In my spirit the dumb lament,
Invincible iniquity: dissolve them.

From remorse, howl without end,
In the unutterable dark
Claustral terror,
Redeem me, raise
Your merciful lashes from your long sleep.

Engendering mind, raise once more
Your rose-coloured unexpected sign,
And take me by surprise again.
Unhoped for, yet arise
O unbelievable dimension, peace;

In the soaring landscape make it so
That I may once more spell out simple words.

The Angel of the Poor*

Now that darkened minds are invaded by
Harsher pity of blood and of the earth,
Now at each heartbeat we are measured by
The silence of so many unjust deaths,

Now the angel of the poor awakes,
Gentleness in the soul, that has survived . . .

With the undying gesture of the centuries
He comes down to lead his ancient people
In the thick of shadows . . .

*One of the series *I Ricordi*, dated 1942–6. The next poem, 'Cry Out
No More', also belongs to the series. Ungaretti returned to Italy in
1942, when the country was about to pay the price of fascism.

Cry Out No More

Stop killing the dead,
Cry out no more, do not cry out
If you wish still to hear them,
If you hope not to perish.

Their whisper is imperceptible,
They make no more noise
Than the growth of grass,
Happy where no man passes.

Variations on Nothing

That nothing nothingness of sand that runs
Dumbly from the hourglass and sifts down,
And, momentary, the imprints on the flesh,
On the dying complexion, of a cloud . . .

Then a hand that turns the hourglass over,
The return, the stirring, of the sand,
The unsounded silvering of a cloud
At the first brief glimmerings of dawn . . .

The hand, in shadow, turned the hourglass over,
And that nothingness of sand running
Silently, is all we can still hear,
And that, being heard, does not go down to darkness.

Last Choruses for the Promised Land*

I

Leeched upon today
All past days
And those to come.

For years and the length of centuries
Surprise at every instant
To know we are still alive,
That living still flows on as always,
Unexpected gifts and griefs
In the continual whirl
Of pointless changes.

Such by our destiny
Is the journey I am making,
In the winking of an eyelid
Unearthing, inventing
Time from top to bottom,
A refugee like all the rest
Who were, who are, who will be.

If at the point where one day meets the others
I come back still intent to find myself
And choose that moment,
It will make house in my soul for ever.

*Dated 1952–60, these are included in *Il Taccuino del Vecchio* (The
Old Man's Notebook). They do not really constitute a series. A
number of the poet's favourite themes – death, the desert, his dead
son, old age, etc. – will be recognized in them.

The person, or the object or event
Or unfamiliar or familiar places
That roused that passion in me, or that anguish,
Or mindless ecstasy
Or a firm friendship
Are now unchangeable, and part of me.

But will my life, now given to nothing else,
Growing from fear to fear,
Enlarging the emptiness, crowded with shadows
That stay to taunt it with the last
Desires of the pulse,
Will it be forced to watch
The desert spreading
Till it deprive me of
Even memory's savage charity?

3
When one day leaves you, think
Of the next one coming.

For birth is full of promises
Though it is painful,
And the experience of each day reveals
That in binding, loosing or enduring
Days are nothing but a wisp of smoke.

4
We flee towards our destination:
Who will know it?

It is not Ithaca we dream of
Lost in a changing sea,

But our gaze goes to Sinai over the sands
That metes out tedious days.

5
We cross the desert with some last remains
Of a former image in our minds,

Of the Promised Land a living man
Knows nothing more.

6
If our journey lasted to eternity
It would not last an instant, death
Is here already, just before it.

An interrupted instant,
One life on earth can last no longer.

If a man cease upon some Sinai's peak,
For those who stay the law will be renewed,
Illusion become pitiless again.

7
If with one hand you skirt misfortune,
With the other you find
That this is not the whole, if not of ruins.

Surviving till you die: is that living?

One hand holds out against your destiny,
But look, the other tells you

That you can grasp nothing
But crumbs of memory.

8

I often wonder
What you and I were like before.

Were we perhaps the wandering dupes of sleep?

Were those things that we achieved
Done in our sleep, in those times?

Far from each other, in an aurora of echoes,
And while you are reborn in me I hear
In the humming air, that you are waking from
A sleep that foresaw us long ago.

9

Each year, while I am finding out that February
Is sensitive, and dark from modesty,
With tiny flowers the mimosa bursts
Yellow. It is pictured in the window
Of that old house where I used to live,
Also of this, where my last years are passing.

As I draw nearer to the enormous silence,
Will it be a sign that nothing dies
As long as its appearance keeps returning?

Or, at the end, will I learn that death
Reigns over nothing but appearances?

10

Troubles you have hidden from me in your eyes,
So that I see nothing but the restless
Movement, in your lonely rest at night,
Of your remembering limbs,
Add still more shadows to my accustomed darkness,
More than ever they make me nothing but night,
In the dumb shriek, night.

11

It is mist, it drifts and flows, your absence,
It is hope that wears out hope.

Far from you, in the branches I no longer
Hear the whispers that lavish forth the leaves
With untried voices,
When you inflict upon my lifeless fibres
Scorches of spring.

12

To the turned back of a saddened man the west
Offers its spreading tarnishes of blood,
That from the bottom of nights of memory
When salvaged, in the void
Will soon be isolated.
They will bleed alone.

13

Secret rose, you bud out over the abysses
Just as long as I am startled, remembering
As of a sudden, odours
While the lament is raised.

The miracle evoked then blends that night
With that other night for me
When I pursued, to lose you and to find you,
Dashed from the height of freedom
Down into scalding facts,
The dazzle and the rending.

14

It is like the growing light
Or at the zenith: love.

If by a single instant
It moves beyond its noon
Then you may call it death.

15

If sensuousness clutches them
In the desperate search for light,
He sees her as a cloud
Insatiably cutting through
A crush of storms, restraints.

16

Between this star and that one
Night shuts itself away
In a measureless whirling void,

From this star-like solitude
To that star-like solitude.

17

To shine unseen
By the bewildered spaces where
The stars spend immemorial life
Maddened by the weight of solitude.

18

To bear the light, the lash of it,
If the light appears,

To bear the light, to gaze
Unblinking at it,
I train you to suffering,
I expiate your guilt,

In order to bear the light
I set the lash against it,
And read an omen that, however terrible,
Ours will become sublime joy.

19

Let sleep and waking end, from my tired flesh
Because of a healing touch of yours
May endless pang be absent.

20

If you were once more ignorant of the hours,
May it not be that you will feel once more
The trembling that made you in an instant
Happy, rid of soul?

21

Could it be that you'll be once again
Without knowledge of evil, child?

With eyes that see nothing
Except, as it gushes into light,
The spring's chaste restlessness?

22

It is breathless, evening, unbreathable,
If you, my dead, and the few alive I love
Do not come to mind
To bring me good, when
Being alone, I understand, at evening.

23

In this century of patience
And of anguished haste,
In the vaulted sky that is doubled down
And more, to make a husk, and that at will
Makes us minimal or limitless,
Flying at a height
Of eight miles you can see
Time whiten and become
A tender morning,
You can, no point of reference
In the space around you
Coming to remind you
That you are being catapulted
At a thousand miles an hour,
Irrepressible curiosity
And fatal will

Forgetting man
Who can never cease to grow
And has grown already to inhuman size,
You can learn how it comes about that one
Man departs, with neither haste nor patience
Peering under veils
As far as the holocaust of the earth at evening.

24

Let the kite grip me in blue talons
And at the sun's peak
Drop me on the sand
Food for crows.

No more I'll bear corruption on my back,
Spotless I shall be for fire,
For the croaking beaks,
For the reeking fangs of jackals.

Then will the bedouin
Rummaging in the sand
With his stick, discover
A pure white skeleton.

25*

Moonless over Syracuse the night
Fell and the leaden waters
Reappeared unmoving in their channel,

Alone we passed inside the ruin,

A rope-maker moved from far away.

*In the ancient inhabited caves at Syracuse, there is one where the rope-makers used to ply their trade, and which is called after them.

26

Choked with dying groans it disappears,
Returns, returns again, returns and raves,
And ever deeper within myself I hear it
Come more and more alive,
Clear, loving, beloved, and terrible,
Your dead voice.

27

Love no longer is that storm
That in the glare of night
Not long ago still trapped me
Between insomnia and frenzy,

Flash from a lighthouse
Towards which the old captain
Calmly sails.

More about Penguins

Penguinews, which appears every month, contains details of all the new books issued by Penguins as they are published. From time to time it is supplemented by *Penguins in Print,* which is a complete list of all books published by Penguins which are in print. (There are well over three thousand of these.)

A specimen copy of *Penguinews* will be sent to you free on request, and you can become a subscriber for the price of the postage. For a year's issues (including the complete lists) please send 30p if you live in the United Kingdom, or 60p if you live elsewhere. Just write to Dept EP, Penguin Books Ltd, Harmondsworth, Middlesex, enclosing a cheque or postal order, and your name will be added to the mailing list.

Note: *Penguinews* and *Penguins in Print* are not available in the U. S. A. or Canada

Two volumes in this series

Eugenio Montale
Selected Poems

Since the publication of *Ossi di Seppia,* his first volume
of poems, in 1925, Eugenio Montale has come to be
seen in Italy as 'the poet' of this century. His reputation
is now international.

Truth is the only star Montale has followed. Leaning
neither to the right nor the left, favouring neither the
Catholic Church nor the Communist Party, he has stood
on his own and kept his perception completely clear.
His poetry can be difficult, even obscure: but frequently
it reflects life in a strong, musical diction which has
been compared to that of T. S. Eliot.

Cesare Pavese
Selected Poems*

Cesare Pavese committed suicide in 1950 at the height
of his literary career. Famous as a novelist, he will also
be remembered for his sympathetic poetry, which evokes
traditional, timeless Italian life and expresses profound
disquiet at the encroachment of soulless urbanization.
This collection illustrates his deepening preoccupation
with man's isolation and includes two of his most
important essays on poetry.

*Not for sale in the U.S.A.